Restreaming

Restreaming

Thriving in the
Currents of
Retirement

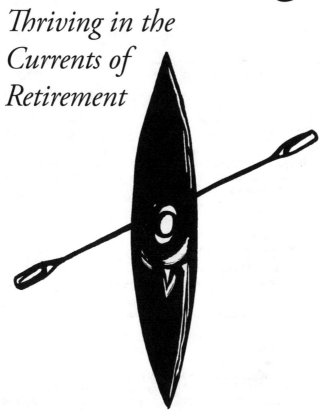

William S. Craddock Jr.

Church Publishing
NEW YORK

Church Publishing
19 East 34th Street
New York, NY 10016
www.churchpublishing.org

Cover art by Maysey Craddock
Cover design by Jennifer Kopec, 2Pug Design
Typeset by Denise Hoff

Library of Congress Cataloging-in-Publication Data

Names: Craddock, William S., author.
Title: Restreaming : thriving in the currents of retirement /
    William S. Craddock Jr.
Description: New York : Church Publishing, 2017.
Identifiers: LCCN 2017008778 (print) | LCCN 2017030412
    (ebook) | ISBN 9780898690040 (ebook) | ISBN 9780898690033 (pbk.)
Subjects: LCSH: Retirement--Planning. | Quality of life.
Classification: LCC HQ1062 (ebook) | LCC HQ1062 .C73 2017 (print)
    | DDC 306.3/8--dc23
LC record available at https://lccn.loc.gov/2017008778

Printed in the United States of America

Contents

Preface

Many people are terrified of the word "retirement" and the relentless march of time into the later years of life. There seems to be a plethora of haunting and persistent questions on their horizon:

"Who am I in this new context of aging and senior status?"
"How am I going to spend the last chapters of my life?"
"What kind of relationships will foster and enrich my
    later years?"
"Are there new ideas, interests, directions I can pursue?"
"How can I make a difference and contribute to the
    lives of others?"

As perceived by many people, the idea of retirement is a radical departure from a previous identity as someone who is making an expected and acceptable contribution in the workplace, and even more basic, being "gainfully" employed with an important role in society. The word retirement is defined simply as the point when a person stops working completely. The idea of retirement emerged in the late nineteenth century when life expectancy was increased and pension plans were introduced. Before then, most continued to work until death. Now there are ten thousand Baby Boomers retiring every day and they will be living longer, in better health, and seeking ways to give back to their community in time, experience, and wealth.

In a recent research article in *Harvard Business Review,*

responders used a variety of metaphors when talking about retirement. Some of the most frequent responses included thinking of retirement as a time to detox from work stress, downshifting from a demanding career, a renaissance opportunity, or even a transformation in their lives. Frederick Houston, in his book *The Adult Years*, suggests that this stage in life is "pro-tirement" when we move ahead into activities that contribute to the best years of our life.

After being retired for over two years, I have experienced in varying degrees all of these feelings, but my favorite metaphor is the kayak. In the past I had often reflected on the metaphor of being in a canoe paddling furiously on one side and then the other in the swift upstream career current—trying to meet other's expectations, deadlines, and time commitments. There was no or little time to turn around and see what kind of wake I was leaving behind me. There was no or little time to sense and feel the deep undercurrent beneath me. There was no or little time to slow down and enjoy the shoreline, the foliage growing, the birds, the clouds above me.

> Rivers know this: there is no hurry. We shall get there some day.
>
> —Winnie-the-Pooh

Since retirement my canoe metaphor has faded. I discovered an opportunity to portage to a gentler, downstream current and my canoe has morphed into a kayak. Instead of resigning myself to a waiting game until I die, I have restreamed, flowing peacefully (most of the time!) into new opportunities, new relationships, new ways of being. My life has become more free, open, and evolving. I now have the opportunity to enjoy my surroundings, reflect on past experiences, and sense the deep undercurrents carrying me forward.

For age is opportunity no less
than youth itself
though in another dress,
and as evening twilight fades away
the sky is filled with stars,
invisible by the day.

—Henry Wadsworth Longfellow

Like the current of a stream, our life is a continuum with everything we have become and all of our relationships that have floated along the slowly meandering and maturing stream of our being. We are all, in a mysterious way, on a long arduous journey in search of a wisdom that would give meaning to life. Our experiences, brought to mind again through memories and reflections, inform and enrich us on this sojourn, this river of life. We use analogies, metaphors, and personal stories to ripen the fruits of our inner dialogue.

The first river you paddle runs through the rest of your life. It bubbles up in pools and eddies to remind you who you are.

—Lynn Noel

Retirement (restreaming) is a key transition time, a time to hold on to what we have learned and skills we have developed and to let go of what is not working, what we don't need anymore. It is never too late to redirect our paths, find new tributaries. We are carried forward, relentlessly, as the unseen force of gravity pulls the water downstream.

The autumn years, until the time of the ultimate letting go of all earthly things, can be the real harvest of our lives. We now have the time to reflect on the fruits of life's experiences. We are given the opportunity to move forward into new activities and relationships.

> Study how water flows in a valley stream, smoothly and freely between the rocks. Also learn from holy books and wise people. Everything—even mountains, rivers, plants and trees—should be your teacher.
>
> —Morihei Ueshiba

This book is not intended to be a litany of self-help tips but to serve as an array of provocative reflections that may prepare us with gentle, intentional strokes in guiding our kayak on our life journey and to thrive in our later years. As I wrote these reflections, I became keenly aware that words do not fully capture and express experiences and underlying truths. Paraphrasing Rumi, the thirteenth-century Sufist, perhaps words are merely dust on the mirror we call experience. As we look deeply into our past experiences, we can begin to appreciate and learn more about ourselves and how we can live meaningfully in our later years.

In looking back at various experiences in my life, I have tried to reflect and write about what I could glean that was worth sharing with others. Perhaps the vignettes in this little book will inspire the reader to pause and reflect on their own experiences—the twists, turns, rocks, rapids, and waterfalls of their river of life within.

I hope you will approach this book like you enjoy a cup of hot coffee or tea early in the morning—taking little sips at a time and savoring the flavor and the thoughts that arise in the stillness and silence of the morning dawning. Each vignette can become a thought or a theme to carry with you through your day.

> Where we find ourselves just now has come out of a series of choices, of streams and rivers taken and not taken, of many right decisions, which have been blessed by God, and wrong decisions, which are being redeemed by God, and that has made all the difference.
>
> —Brother Curtis Almquist, SSJE

The Kayak

Imagine that you are in a kayak floating gently down a cool, clear stream. The kayak is much more stable and balanced than a canoe—flexible, agile, swift, and easy to steer with its two-bladed paddle. When approaching rapids in a canoe, one is anxious to avoid the "Vs" in the stream—telltale signs for submerged rocks. The swift current propels the canoe quickly through the white water. With the one-bladed paddle there is only limited control of direction and speed. In a kayak rapids are approached with much more confidence since one can maneuver in and around the rocks and actually "play" in the turbulent waves and eddies.

As we begin our journey, embrace this kayak metaphor and approach the white-water challenges along the way with confidence that you are in a stable, agile, and flexible self that will not only survive but thrive on this journey. Your fears are mitigated and possibly diminished by your balanced approach and adaptive perspective. There are companions along the way in their own kayaks, floating down, negotiating the rapids and rocks on their own journeys. The swift current of time will carry you through difficult and challenging obstacles. Stay alert and attentive to the deep undercurrent that may guide you along in God's providential ways of being. Enjoy the ride!

A journey is a person in itself; no two are alike. And all plans, safeguards, policing, and coercion are fruitless. We find that after years of struggle that we do not take a trip; a trip takes us.

—John Steinbeck

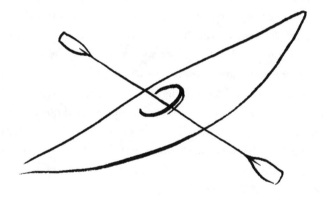

Balancing Life

The kayak is known for its balance—even the word "kayak" is a palindrome, a word that is the same when spelled backwards. A kayak *looks* like a palindrome—the bow and stern are almost identical and one can often only tell the front from the back by the alignment of the seat. Segments of our stream of life are quiet, placid, slow-moving. Other parts are challenging as we are surrounded with chaotic white waters. Our journey will have a balance of both contentments and challenges.

As we enter retirement, a critical key is to craft a life that is balanced—not too much "taking it easy" but not too much "staying real busy." Shifting from a work pattern of "nine-to-five" with its demands and expectations to a retirement pattern with almost no structure can be frightening. In the first few months of my "restreaming," I began to realize that I could not just drift along in the easy, comfortable current of homeostasis. I needed to find a balance between contentment and challenge. I was eager to engage in the life around me and find ways I could give back to others and to my community.

Recent studies indicate that a moderate amount of stress (called eustress) lights up our brain circuits and focuses our attentions and awareness of life around us. We are at our best when engaged in an array of external activities, projects, and relationships, and also taking "time out" for solitude and reflection.

Happiness is not a matter
of intensity but of balance,
order, rhythm and harmony.

—Thomas Merton

Morning Dawning

Morning dawn happens when the sun is less than six degrees below the horizon and the rays of sunlight silently and slowly scatter across the sky. There is a pristine and sacred stillness in these early moments of solitude.

In the very early morning, the only conversation is with myself and with God. In younger times in my life, there was the chatter of children, time commitments, and worries about work, but now, in retirement. . . . ah, yes, the silence that invites reflections into a deeper sense of being!

Imagine the shape of the opening day and wonder where you will find yourself in it. Floating in the gentle current of your journey stream, you may become aware that you will be directed by an array of choices, moment by moment. Every time a choice is made, your life, your identity, your relationships will be changed. So what choices, what decisions will you make in the morning dawning that align with your deepest passions, that will spring fresh from the Word?

> Morning has broken, like the first morning,
> Blackbird has spoken, like the first bird.
> Praise for the singing! Praise for the morning!
> Praise for them, springing fresh from the Word!
>
> —Eleanor Farjeon

Silent Undercurrent

The light went out. I was scuba diving deep in a cold, dark limestone cave in Florida, alone, when my underwater flashlight was crushed by the pressure of eighty feet of water. As a twenty-year-old college student on a spring fling, I was stupid and reckless to be diving into an underground cave with a fresh water river coursing through the limestone. The water had been crystal clear as I eased through the mouth of the cave, admiring the slippery, fresh-water eels darting through little openings and crevices.

When the light went out, I somehow didn't panic. I knew that if I was very still the river current would gently take me to the mouth of the cave and to the light of the outside world. In a few seconds, I could see the cave's opening and the sun's light shining through the water. I was safe, alive, relieved, and strangely humbled.

As I reflect on this foolish experience of my youth, I think about the importance of being still and letting God's unseen but powerful "current" carry me forward to the light of Life. At other times in my life, I have experienced this deep and silent undercurrent that has swept me along in God's providential ways of being.

Be still, and know that I am God!

—Psalms 46:10

Turning Points

It was just a casual question. I was standing in the kitchen of a good friend's home at her dinner party when I asked if she could recommend some recent theologians and their writings. I was in my early forties. I had family responsibilities with a wife, three daughters, their schools and activities. I had business commitments with financial obligations and employees whose livelihood depended on me.

Consciously, I wasn't aware that I was searching for a way to "get away from the rat race" and shift careers. But deep down I could sense a faint but growing passion for a deeper understanding of my identity and my relationship with God.

She looked straight at me and replied, "Why don't you read the Bible?"

I laughed nervously, not really sure where she was going with this question.

Her follow-up question was "Why don't you sign up for EfM?" EfM, or Education for Ministry, is a four-year Episcopal learning certificate program in theological education, based upon small-group study and practice.

Two months later I walked into my first EfM class. It was a group of ten people of all ages and walks of life. I quickly realized that this community was radically different from the business groups and civic organizations I had previously experienced. These people were authentic, intimate, and seemed to possess an emotional maturity and a devotion to God. I was deeply touched and humbled to be in their company.

After completing the four years of EfM along with considerable soul-searching discernment, I was able to leave the business world and begin a meandering, challenging, and rewarding career with the Episcopal Church. Yes, it was important to have enough money to make ends meet but more important to seize the opportunity to make meaning in other people's lives. I was given the wonderful opportunity to become a meaning-maker more than a money-maker.

It may be superficial to reflect on one episode and claim it was a turning point in my life, but, upon reflection, my casual question in my friend's kitchen "kick-started" a major shift in my life and that has made all the difference. Everyone has significant turning points (forks in our streams) that send us in new directions. Retirement is a significant turning point offering opportunities to move in new directions with new attitudes, new relationships, new dreams.

> To exist is to change; to change is to mature;
> to mature is to create oneself endlessly.
>
> —Henri Bergson

Downshifting

When my oldest daughter was beginning to learn to drive, I bought an old blue MGB convertible. It had a manual transmission. When she was about to turn sixteen, I took her to a large parking lot every day for several days and we practiced shifting with the manual transmission. There were four steps in the downshift sequence:

1. Take foot off the gas pedal.

2. Push clutch down to the floor.

3. Shift stick to next lower gear.

4. Ease off the clutch while slowly pressing the gas pedal.

It took a lot of patience with some jerky moments of clutch-popping, before she got the hang of it. Downshifting is proven to be an efficient and safer way to slow down the car without overusing the brakes.

In our retirement years, we are encouraged to "downshift" too. Social scientists have used this terminology to describe a social behavior in which individuals shift to simpler lives with more balanced time for leisure, for building relationships, for pursuing new interests. Downshifting as a concept suggests a gradual slowing down using a "lower" gear.

Just as my daughter had to practice in a large parking lot how to downshift, as we enter our retirement years, we will need to practice downshifting and in a metaphorical way follow the four steps in the downshift sequence. It will involve a variety of behavioral and lifestyle changes but if approached with practice and patience, these changes will be gradual, moderate, and in the long run, life-giving. We will be able to slow down our lives and make the mornings last.

> Slow down, you move too fast
> You got to make the morning last.
> Just kicking down the cobble stones
> Looking for fun and feelin' groovy.
>
> —Lyrics by Simon and Garfunkel

A Sense of the Sacred

> A person should hear a little music, read a little poetry,
> and see a fine picture every day in order that worldly
> cares may not obliterate the sense of the beautiful
> which God has implanted in the human soul.
>
> —Johann Wolfgang von Goethe

Quiet, still, silent, and yet deep with expression—those were the swirling feelings as I stood in the Rothko Chapel in front of fourteen massive black paintings with hues of deep blue and maroon colors. Time was seemingly suspended and there was a profound experience that surpassed or exceeded the aesthetic and drew me into an intimate "non-place" of authentic spirituality.

My wife and I had been in Houston to make a difficult visit with a friend and, on the spur of the moment, decided to go to the Rothko Chapel, a nondenominational octagonal building in a middle-class suburb. We discovered that this little chapel was a holy place open to all religions and belonging to none. There were several benches for meditative seating and many were filled with visitors from various ethnic backgrounds. As we entered the stone chapel, there was a startling sense of the sacred.

Mark Rothko, an American painter of Russian Jewish descent, had moved through a series of phases and art movements over his life. In his later years, he expressed his intentions to "make art as an adventure into an unknown world and relieve modern man's

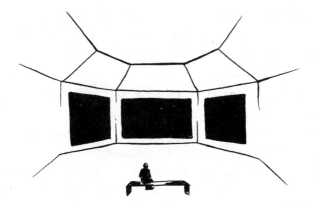

spiritual emptiness by favoring the simple expression of the complex thought." He wanted to create a space of human consciousness that transcends specific history and culture.

As I sat on a bench quietly staring at these large blocks of dark colors, I was overwhelmed by the feeling that these paintings were somehow windows into my deepest thoughts and soul. The luminous colors on the large, rectangular panels provoked an array of human emotions and a sense of the sacred.

Adaptation

In retirement, we may perceive ourselves as "old dogs" with no flexibility or inclination to take on new tricks. When presented with new situations, we are sometimes reluctant or slow to leave our "comfort zone."

There was a moment in the first week after I retired when I really felt awkward and, frankly, embarrassed. Somewhat lost, I was wandering through the aisles of the local grocery store looking for various items on a long list my wife had given me. Jim, a good friend I have known for years, was also cart-pushing with a handful of coupons. When he saw me, his face broke into a broad, self-assured smile.

Jim had retired a few years ago and seemed to know the grocery store landscape like the back of his hand. He knew of my recent retirement and must have seen the lost and embarrassed look on my face as I stumbled my way through the aisles. He laughed, took my cart, and guided me through the store picking up listed items with efficient ease. After checking out, we shared a cup of coffee and talked about the awkward, fish-out-of-water feelings of early retirement. Over the past year, I have adapted to a new rhythm and no longer feel embarrassed about not being "at work" in the middle of the day. Also, I am pleased to know my way around the grocery store and can even keep up with the wad of saving coupons.

A major contributor to our health and well-being in our later years is our ability to adapt to the shifting sands and swirling streams underneath our kayak. To negotiate the rapid and chaotic changes in our lives, we need to be alert, agile, and adaptive—continually pursuing our best options, modifying our behavior to "fit better" in our new environment. There are habits and routines to give up and better ones to begin.

Too often we fall back on habits, attitudes, and relationships that have worked well in past experiences. How we respond to the forces of change will depend on our willingness and capacity to adapt.

> I left the woods for as good a reason as I went there. Perhaps it seemed to me that I had several more lives to live and could not spare any more time for that one.
>
> —Henry David Thoreau

Joy

The end of a calendar year is a superficial yet noteworthy marker in our lives. It's a good time to reflect on the past twelve months and welcome a new year possibly with new habits, hopes, and directions.

I have used this marked time to reflect on what brought me joy in the past year. The list is different every year but the patterns, themes, and origins of joy have been similar. My joyful moments have been spontaneous, relational, without monetary costs, and wrapped with love.

Making dye-colored pancakes with grandchildren, walking in woods with a close friend, enjoying a cool glass of white wine with my wife in the back yard, listening to a Bach prelude at the beginning of church, the list goes on and on.

Joy is defined as exhilaration, delight, sheer gladness, heightened sense of well-being, feeling of great pleasure, elation. One of the best expressions of joy in the Bible is in 2 Samuel 6:5—"*David and all the house of Israel were dancing before the Lord with all their might . . . .*" Although we don't have a physical ark to celebrate and dance around, we do have metaphorical arks in nature and in the people in our lives that give us great joy.

We cannot "skate" through life with overly enthusiastic, Pollyanna attitudes. We need to be realists confronting life's struggles with focus and determination, but at the same time, be aware and indulge in the joys that can come our way every day.

Being attentive and alert to the delightful wonders that appear in our lives will enhance our sense of well-being and strengthen our resolve to live life fully and joyfully.

You've gotta dance like there's nobody watching,
Love like you'll never be hurt,
Sing like there's nobody listening,
And live like it's heaven on earth.

—William W. Purkey

The Deep Current

We know the current is there—it is only seen in its movement. We know from our life experience the wisdom of living with the subtle but keen awareness of the deep currents in our lives. Running beneath the surface of our sense-driven experiences is the deeper and truer life waiting to be acknowledged and embraced. It's deeper than our linear logic paths, deeper than our ego, much deeper.

This deep current cannot be brought to the surface but can be followed and intuited from our kayak on the surface. The current of life carries us resolutely along. We stare at its deepness, and slowly thoughts drift along like our paddle ripples—quietly dissipating until they arrive at the riverbank.

Albert Einstein once said, "Look deep, deep into nature and then you will understand everything." Perhaps it's bold to question Dr. Einstein, but if we look deep into nature, look deep into the undercurrent of our life, it will allow us to begin to understand ourselves.

> Late, by myself, in the boat of myself,
> no light and no land anywhere,
> cloudcover thick. I try to stay
> just above the surface, yet I'm already under
> and living within the ocean.
>
> —Rumi

Sweet Spots

In sports we have all heard of the phrase "hitting the sweet spot." It's a place where the ball strikes the racket, bat, or club in the ideal spot for providing the maximum positive impact and momentum.

There are times early in our life when we have all hit a sweet spot—the first time we rode a bicycle down a driveway, built a model airplane, or aced a test.

Mihaly Csikszentmihalyi, an esteemed psychologist, wrote the book *Flow: The Psychology of Optimal Experience*. He observed that people feel happy, alive, and fulfilled when they can "forget" themselves and are completely absorbed in an activity. They are totally immersed in the flow of the moment, not even aware of the time or even a conscious self.

If we are observant and attentive in our retirement years, we can experience an array of different sweet spots—celebrating a grandchild's graduation from kindergarten, making a cherry pie for someone who has been ill, writing a poem, walking in a park on a cool fall day with a close friend. It is in these explored moments, these sweet spots, that we are not life spectators but actively engaged, feeling creative, alive, filled with joy and in the flow.

Fear

Studies have confirmed that when exposed to fear, our brains, imaged by an fMRI scanner, light up in the right amygdala, a part of the brain related to fight-or-flight fear response. Fear is inbred in us—it's a standardized biological reaction.

In early childhood our fears may have been of ghoulies and ghosties and long-legged beasties, or a bully in the neighborhood, or our mother leaving us alone. In adolescence we may have feared not fitting in, poor grades, or making the team. In mid-life our fears may have shifted as we became anxious about our job, fears of failure, fears for our children's health and success. In our later years, studies have indicated that our fears have shifted again.

When my father was in his late eighties, he told me that he wasn't afraid of death but feared the process of dying. Wrapped up in this fear is a complex package of anxious uncertainties including health, self-autonomy, loneliness, in addition to ego death or extinction.

We all have experienced fears in our lives. What matters is how we cope with them. If only we could make a list of our fears and construct rational strategies to deal with them. Most of our fears are lingering in the vague world of our imagination. Since they swirl around in our mind and very rarely present themselves in the real world, it's difficult to address fears in a methodical, "fix-it" way.

Contextuality is a counterweight to fear. Perhaps the best approach would be to practice a balanced perspective that places our fears in a framework of our whole life. When we pause to take count of our many blessings and fully engage in our vital relationships with loved ones, families, friends, and with God, our fears and anxieties may fade away. Engaging life with hope and a focus on strengthening relationships may be the best antidote to our fears and anxieties.

> do not fear, for I am with you, do not be afraid, for I am your God; I will strengthen you, I will help you, I will uphold you with my victorious right hand.
>
> —Isaiah 41:10

> When you pass through the waters, I will be with you; and through the rivers, they shall not overwhelm you . . .
>
> —Isaiah 43:2

Vehicles for Relationships

My grandfather was short in stature but tall in kindness and integrity. He was a quiet, humble man with a keen mind and an uncanny ability to quote Shakespeare at the drop of a hat. Often, on weekends, he would buy lemon layer cakes from the local bakery and we would take them to friends who were sick or down on their luck. On summer evenings we would sit on his porch after dinner with bowls of his favorite ice cream listening to the cicadas while his cigar smoke kept the mosquitoes at bay.

One summer evening when I had returned from college, I asked him what career path I should pursue in my life. I will never forget his response. He chuckled lightly and leaned over to me with a wide smile and said, "It's certainly important to follow your interests, your passions, but more important for you to pay attention to relationships. After all, your future career is really a vehicle for relationships."

As I look back on my "careers" over the past almost fifty years, the highlights are not tied to the money made, the deals consummated, the prestige projects completed. The most significant and meaningful recollections are the people I have known, the relationships that have enriched and deepened my life in so many ways. And now, in retirement, I have an even deeper appreciation of friends, family, and even new relationships.

The local bakery that sold the lemon layer cakes is gone as is my grandfather, but his words of advice continue to guide me and my kayak into nurturing old and cultivating new relationships as I continue my journey of life.

Cross-Training

As a young adult I took up running and there were big changes—in my weight, conditioning, endurance, and even my attitude and outlook on life. I discovered that my daily run was a way I could combat stress and "clear" my mind of troublesome worries and problems. Studies have confirmed that exercise can reduce anxiety and depression by immediate increases in levels of key neurotransmitters including serotonin, noradrenalin, dopamine, and endorphins. We can even live longer and have more positive, healthy lives with regular exercise.

After ten years of competing in road races and marathons, my body broke down with numerous ailments and injury. Daily exercise, however, had become a healthy habit and an important part of my day. I began cross-training, a balanced mix of aerobic exercises, to work various parts of my body and muscle groups. I worked with a swim coach to hone my stroke technique and joined a Masters Swimming club. I didn't join a yoga group but learned basic yoga positions through various online instructors and started "doing" yoga in my home. A trainer worked with me with a weight lifting routine at a local fitness center.

Varying these exercise routines every day strengthened my body and eliminated chronic injuries caused by my previous focus on running. Cross-training with a variety of exercises and stimuli has kept my workouts fresh and exciting.

I recall as a young child late at night turning the dials on my crystal radio and listening to music on different stations. There was always a feeling of delight to stumble across a new song or one that I had heard before and over time had become a favorite. Turning our spiritual dials through various exercises can allow us to "tune into" a deeper understanding of ourselves and our relationship with God. Spiritual cross-training in a variety of ways such as contemplative prayer, lectio divina, meditation, Bible study, and even just listening to choral music can offer a more balanced and healthy spiritual life.

Letting Go

Two monks, going to a neighboring monastery, walked side by side in silence. They arrived at a river they had to cross. That season, waters were higher than usual. On the bank, a young woman was hesitating and asked the younger of the two monks for help. He exclaimed, "Don't you see that I am a monk, that I took a vow of chastity?"

"I require nothing from you that could impede your vow, but simply to help me to cross the river," replied the young woman with a little smile.

"I . . . not . . . I can . . . do nothing for you," said the embarrassed young monk.

"It doesn't matter," said the elderly monk. "Climb on my back and we will cross together."

Having reached the other bank, the old monk put down the young woman who, in return, thanked him with a broad smile. She left and both monks continued their route in silence. Close to the monastery, the young monk could not stand it anymore and said, "You shouldn't have carried that person on your back. It's against our rules."

> "This young woman needed help and I put her down on the other bank. You didn't carry her at all, but she is still on your back," replied the older monk.
>
> —Zen Buddhist Story

One of the great challenges in the art of life is to learn how to let things go. We have all tried to learn how to avoid letting our anger, our frustration, our resentment, our disagreements not get the best of us, not to "make our day."

I remember sitting in a church meeting in my early thirties watching two elderly men going at each other over some minor church-related issue. The following Sunday I was sitting, as I always do, in the back of the church as everyone stood up by rows and walked to the altar for communion. These two men happened to be sitting on opposite rows and as they approached the aisle, they briefly held hands and smiled before walking together to take communion. This was an important and lasting lesson for me. They had learned to "let things go" and move on without carrying the heavy burdens of previous angst and even anger on their backs. A deeper lesson was the sacred, unseen power of communion in drawing them and all of us together in love for each other.

> Some of us think holding on makes us strong; but sometimes it is letting go.
>
> —Hermann Hesse

A Rhythm of REP

At some time or another, each of us is confronted with change, stress, isolation, emotional labor, physical conditions, and little time to nurture our own spiritual nourishment and care. Studies have indicated that the three "plagues" of old age are boredom, loneliness, and helplessness. Although there will always be hints and whiffs of these plagues in our later years, we can mitigate and even become immune to them by integrating an REP rhythm.

Acronyms are helpful in remembering a series of words, and this one, REP, serves as a valuable framework for our restreamed kayak. The renewal of our journey in retirement is keyed on three things:

» Relationship—a sense of connectedness with others and mutual caring. Many recent studies have confirmed the importance of having a wide variety of relationships and support groups. We are relational beings and thrive when we are in the company of others.

» Exercise—active and regular engagement of physical, mental, and spiritual practices. When someone keeps moving, keeps physically fit, their mental attitude and outlook on life is much more positive. Also, we must "exercise" our minds, seeking new areas of learning and finding methods to break away from routines and old ways of thinking.

» Purpose—making a difference, creating meaning on our journey. It has been said that "as the body cannot live without food, the soul cannot live without meaning." Making a meaningful difference in others' lives can positively impact our own sense of self and deepen our understanding and appreciation of our life with each other.

Sometimes we have high expectations of what life ought to give us, but usually we don't get everything we want. Life doesn't accommodate us, it challenges us. We cannot sit around and wait for good things to happen to us, we need to actively pursue the "REPs," throwing ourselves wholeheartedly into each of these life-giving areas.

If opportunity doesn't knock, build a door.

—Milton Berle

Going with the Flow

Many years ago my family went out west for a summer vacation. One of the highlights was a raft trip down a swiftly moving river with plenty of rapids and white waters. Before launching our rafts, we sat on the bank with our helmets, life preservers, and paddles listening intently to our guide's instructions. I recall his advice to allow the flow of the water to guide the raft through the rocks and boulders in the rapid sections. Don't try to paddle to avoid the rocks. The river's current will float the raft along the course but always, always keep the raft facing forward.

At the time this advice seemed counterintuitive. Common sense was to paddle away from danger. Following the guide's advice was important and we successfully and safely floated down the river.

Our journey of life is a similar sojourn—we can't effectively avoid the hardships and challenges confronting us. We must courageously face forward and learn to "go with the flow," allowing the current of life to guide us through the hard knocks and rocks in our life. We can't push the current or make the river go a certain way. We can paddle to one side or the other, even pull on shore for a while.

The river keeps flowing. Life keeps changing. What we can do is stay alert, awake, enjoy the ride, and gracefully allow the river to carry us.

I would love to live
Like a river flows
Carried by the surprise
Of its unfolding.

      —John O'Donahue

Being Aware of the Present

Some years ago, in a taxi in New York City, stuck in traffic, I was suddenly aware that the driver was smiling and humming to himself. I asked him why he was so happy in the midst of this snarling gridlocked mess with honking horns and hot tempers. He turned around and said: "Mister . . . yesterday is history, tomorrow is a mystery, today is a gift of God, which is why we call it the present. We should all be grateful to be present here today." (I later learned that this phrase is attributed to American cartoonist Bil Keane.)

The present is where the past and future intersect. It doesn't really exist by itself. We experience being in the present in a participatory way—not thinking about it but being in the moment. The challenge however is that too much of the day we are pondering the past or imagining the future and not truly being in the present.

On our imaginary kayak journey in our retirement stream, we should lift up our two-bladed paddles and prop them on the kayak's gunwales. Drift along and be aware of the present. Sometimes it isn't easy. Our hearts may be too heavy from past experiences and losses. Our thoughts may be anxious with the challenges looming in our future. Yet, we have the privilege of living in the moment and seeing the lilies of the field, the birds in the trees, the surface of the water occasionally and silently roiling with a fish just below. Living in the present is a gift, receive it gladly and rejoice.

> In today's rush, we all think too much—seek too much—want too much—and forget about the joy of just being.
>
> —Eckhart Tolle

Keeping Busy
or Keeping in Touch

At a local restaurant, an old friend ran into me and casually asked how I was keeping busy now that I had retired. I realize that this is a frequent question raised to those who have recently retired and there are probably many ways to respond.

Studies indicate that for a majority of retirees, retirement is understood not as a frenetic phase to "keep busy finding ways to spend time," but more about being, about relationships, about meaning-making, about joy.

One of the preeminent theorists of human developmental psychology was Abraham Maslow. Until recently, his pyramid-shaped hierarchy of needs has been a commonly accepted theory describing the stages of growth in humans. The highest level of Maslow's pyramid was self-actualization, a need to "be all that we can be."

Recently psychologists have questioned Maslow's ranking of needs. They suggest that in the later years people begin to discover a transcendent desire to seek companionship and to help others achieve their potential. There is a desire to explore purposes outside ourselves that are meaningful—that can make a difference in others' lives. We all seek a cause beyond ourselves—this is an intrinsic human need that seems to manifest itself in retirement.

In our imaginary kayak, we are not paddling and drifting downstream all alone. There are others in front, alongside, and behind us. Occasionally, we will be helped by others to navigate the rough waters and other times we will eagerly offer assistance. In this sense of belonging, companionship, and caring for each other, we begin to see ourselves as part of something greater. We are not merely "keeping busy" but "keeping in touch" with our family, with our friends, and with God.

> In early stages, I struggled to make sense of things, make sense of my life. Now I have tilted to make meaning, make a difference, make a contribution to the people in this world.
>
> Joy, rather than happiness, is the goal of life, for joy is the emotion which accompanies our fulfilling our natures as human beings. It is based on the experience of one's identity as a being of worth and dignity.
>
> —Rollo May

Seafood Gumbo

Occasionally, I think I know how to cook. There is one dish that has been a challenge to my culinary skills and patience—seafood gumbo.

The most important ingredient is the roux—a patiently stirred, simmering blend of oil and flour. These two basic ingredients must be carefully measured and simmered in a skillet over medium heat. The roux begins as white pasty goo that slowly darkens and thins after several minutes of stirring. A good roux for gumbo should be a rich dark brown color. That's the challenge—I have to be patient and attentive stirring the roux as it shifts from white to blond to caramel to dark chocolate in color. Once the roux is rich and dark, the recipe is easy. I just throw into the pot handfuls of celery, onions, tomatoes, okra, crabs, shrimp, sausage, and anything else I can find. I put a lid on the pot and just let it simmer for hours. Served with rice . . . *Laissez les bons temps rouler!*

Restreaming

Some dreams and visions in our life come together in a way similar to this gumbo recipe. The initial, early stages take time and require patience and attention. Some ideas gel when slowly simmering in our minds and hearts in what can be called creative worrying. After a while of sorting out options and impacts on our life and those of others, a dream can evolve into a concept and morph into a plan that can be implemented. We can move from a vague and ambiguous imagination to a rich, "dark chocolate" reality. With a carefully thought-out strategy, the details and implementation can be much easier and effective.

Whether we are cooking up a pot of gumbo or a pot of new dreams, we need to be patient, attentive, and trust the slow work of our simmering roux.

Center of the Universe

Nicolaus Copernicus in the sixteenth century developed a model in which the Earth and other planets revolve around the Sun. This heliocentric theory was opposed to the ancient geocentric belief that the heavens revolved around the earth. Since Copernicus's discovery, there has been an expansion of his model to include elliptical orbits, discoveries of other galaxies, and recently, with Einstein's principle of relativity, astronomers and mathematicians conclude that there is no specific location that is the center of the universe.

Infants see themselves as the center of their universe, yet through experience and relationships their perspective slowly expands to include their family and their home. As a person matures and learns to construct and negotiate reality, there is a rational sense that they are really not the center of the universe, but many of their behaviors and practices support a self-centric ontology.

As a Baby Boomer, my early adult life was teeming with a compelling appetite to win, to get ahead, to run the race of my life. This was a phase when I was focused on building a business, providing for my family, running marathons, taking on leadership roles in the community. I was possessed with a merit-badge mentality, focused on a pre-occupation with myself. Looking back on those years, I may have been an Ayn Rand devotee pursuing the virtue of selfishness and feeding my hungry ego needs.

Studies confirm that many of us who "survive" our midlife, ego-driven, competitive years, gradually realize a subtle yet profound paradigm shift. Instead of perceiving life as a race, they see life as a journey. Instead of a focus on getting ahead and pursuing success, they have more energy and interest in engaging in relationships and giving back. Instead of being the center of attention, they are more attentive to the world around them.

We are transformed when we undergo this internal Copernican revolution. A healthy, mature ego provides us with a courageous understanding that the universe does not circle around us. If the astronomers and mathematicians are correct in their claim that there is no specific location that is the center of the universe, perhaps there is something called love that can be found everywhere?

> Peace comes from within the souls of men when they realize their oneness with the Universe.
>
> —Black Elk

> The universe is centered on neither the earth nor the sun, it is centered on God.
>
> —Alfred Noyes

Living Streams

When we think of streams, we assume there are beginnings and endings. The headwaters of a stream could be an underground river, a watershed from a high plain or mountain. Streams appear to be living waters, constantly moving, enriching the biodiverse life along its course. Streams are in constant motion with currents continually emptying the water into larger streams, rivers, lakes, and oceans. Each molecule of water is swept eventually into the ocean along with billions of others.

Our life can be viewed as on a journey in a stream. We sense intuitively that we are carried relentlessly along into more experiences. In the early stages of our younger life, the water carries us rapidly and chaotically around rocks, obstacles, over falls, rushing in shallow white-water turbulence.

In the later stages of our life, we have an intuitive sense that the stream slows in a deeper, more gentle current with fewer obstacles and more experienced-based wisdom and confidence. We can see ourselves with many opportunities to engage and enrich others along the way. Our life flows, never ceasing, in the stream until we join, blend, and unite with other streams and pour into the infinite ocean of eternity.

The rivers flow not past, but through us, thrilling, tingling, vibrating every fiber and cell of the substance of our bodies, making them glide and sing.

—John Muir

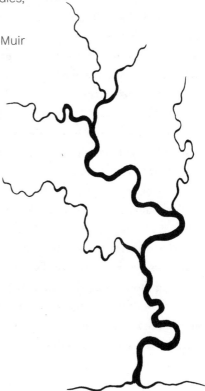

Running in the Park

My best friend, Henry, is a yellow lab with deep brown eyes and a black nose that constantly twitches, catching the multitude of scents in the air. He is twelve years old (eighty-four in dog years) and is getting stiff and arthritic with the incessant punishment of gravity and time. He follows me around the house, lays under my chair and, when not snoring or chasing squirrels in a dream, looks up to me with an insatiable yearning to love and be loved. His aim in dog life is to please and most of the time he achieves his mission.

I used to take Henry to a beautiful, urban virgin forest park in the middle of the city. We would run the trails around vines, over creeks, and through the tall hardwoods—some are over a hundred years old. My initial thoughts were cluttered with the upcoming day's activities but sometimes my thoughts subtly shifted to the awesome beauty of nature in this old forest.

Even though Henry can no longer run with me, in the early mornings I still go to the park. It's a humbling experience to be a retired and aging man slowly jogging in the deep shadows of these enchanting woods. Occasionally, not too often, I sense that my rambling thoughts cohere and join into a beautiful symphony in harmony with the universe surrounding me. It seems to me to be a state of at-one-ment, or an at-one-moment, when I feel that I am merely a very tiny spark in this universe-wide fire of Life.

Days pass and the years vanish and we walk sightless among miracles. Lord, fill our eyes with seeing and our minds with knowing. Let there be moments when your Presence, like lightning, illumines the darkness in which we walk. Help us to see, wherever we gaze, that the bush burns, unconsumed. And we, clay touched by God, will reach out for holiness and exclaim in wonder, "How filled with awe is this place and we did not know it."

—Attributed to Mishkan Tefilah
from the Jewish Sabbath Prayer Book

The Love Field

The physical world around us is perceived and defined through our five senses. In this way we construct and navigate a time- and space-bound reality. It is what we casually assume is our "universe." Some physicists contend that there are numerous worlds "out there" and we are encompassed in multiverses.

Our mind, through its experience and sense-driven rationale, has difficulty comprehending other worlds, multiverses. Using our five senses, these other worlds cannot be seen, heard, tasted, touched, or smelled. However, we all have emotional relationships that are sometimes felt as "another world out there"—a divine field of love. This "love field" can only be felt with the compassionate and emotional language of the heart.

Being in an authentic relationship with one another can occasionally release us from our cerebral machinations and pull us into a deeper appreciation of this force field of love. I recall watching my young grandson score his first soccer goal. He ran quickly off the field with his hands held high and gave me a big celebratory hug of happiness. I am not sure how the physics of this experience works—the pumping of endorphins, the immediate sparking in the amygdala. But I do know that I felt his love and celebrated his goal with a warm embrace and a heart filled with joy. In that moment, our relationship was more meaningful and present than the physical world around us.

Our challenge, as human beings, is to find ways to receive and embrace love and practice infecting others with this love in our physical universe of the five senses.

> The greatest happiness of life is the conviction that we are loved; loved for ourselves, or rather, loved in spite of ourselves.
>
> —Victor Hugo

Anticipatory Emotions

When floating in my imaginary kayak, my random thoughts and emotions float along with me and then . . . something signals me to shift my gaze. I see a subtle swirl in the water ahead. I can imagine, hopefully, whipping my fly rod across the stream, waiting with anticipation for a big trout to lunge at my artificial midge with its tiny hook. Or, fearfully, do I see the fat snout and beady eyes of an alligator submerged just under the water surface staring at me in my kayak? In moments like this, I am really focused, with eyes riveted on the swirl in the water flushed with mixed anticipatory emotions of hope and fear.

A significant contributing factor to our well-being is our ability to understand and manage our emotions. Emotions arise from the limbic system, a part of our primitive brain that allowed our early ancestors to survive. The prototypical affects of hope and fear can impact our decisions and behaviors. Hope provides us with positive energy and good feelings as we anticipate a desirable future event. Fear, associated with undesirable future events, brings up negative thoughts.

Although we cannot control our emotions, we can find ways to manage them. Everyone consciously or unconsciously builds up a repertoire of coping skills that work best for them. There are many healthy ways to cope with our emotions, including exercise, meditation, and social support—all can be effective. Sometimes we fall back to unhealthy responses including alcohol, digital distractions, or even denial and avoidance. If we can recognize our emotions, we can intentionally practice healthy coping behaviors and manage life with more confidence and positive results.

Our life journeys have been peppered with hopes and fears. Whether there is in our future a trout or an alligator, we can pay attention to our emotions and monitor our behavior for the best outcome possible.

Contemplation

Sometimes, we need to moor our kayak on the edge of the stream and observe our own stream of consciousness. Initially in the silence of these moments, random thoughts and emotions assert themselves. A key learning in the practice of contemplation is to become aware that we are not our feelings. With concentration, we can become a "watcher" and observe cascading thoughts and feelings without judgment. We can sit on the banks of the stream and watch thoughts floating along and just let them go down with the current.

In Christian theology, there is a word for this "self-emptying": "kenosis." Like a cup that can only serve as a receptacle if emptied, we can become receptive to God's divine will when we are emptied of our own thoughts and emotions. The word "contemplation" is derived from Old French and originally meant the "act of looking at." Actually, prayers are the quintessence of contemplation—being aware of being in the presence of God.

> See the day begin and lean back, a simple wakefulness filling perfectly the spaces among the leaves.
>
> —Wendell Berry

Radical Amazement

Young children are wonder-filled. Their imagination has not yet been hammered by the hard-edged anvil of reality. Their open-minded approach extends from stockings filled by Santa Claus to flying across pirate ships with Tinkerbell pixie dust.

When my youngest daughter lost a tooth, our family had just nestled down in sleeping bags in a tent at a campsite in Arkansas. She began crying because she thought the tooth fairy wouldn't know she had a tooth under her pillow. I walked over to a pay phone nearby while she watched anxiously through a slit in the tent flap. I called the tooth fairy and explained what happened. The next morning she found a quarter under her pillow and all was well and wonderful.

As we journey through life, for most of us the sense of wonder fades. It's easy to become mired in the muck of a routine life. When we take things for granted, we are missing out on the wonder all about us. Rabbi Abraham Heschel coined the phrase "radical amazement," and comments that "the beginning of happiness lies in the understanding that life without wonder is not worth living."

Can we relearn the radical wonderment of our childhood? Perhaps, in our later years, as we float downstream in our kayak, we can learn to see the world, to see others, to see ourselves as wonderful parts of creation and we will be radically amazed with life.

> Hear this, O Job; stop and consider the wondrous works of God.
>
> —Job 37:14

Working Out

Allan is a retired farmer and works out at the gym every day but Sunday. I am usually there two or three times during the week to do the elliptical and weight machines. Studies have confirmed that lifting weights are essential for healthy muscle tone and flexibility in my senior years.

I call Allan "Coach." He is a bit older than I but has never really been a coach—more like a mentor to me. He calls me "Priest Man," knowing that I used to work with the Episcopal Church but was never ordained into the priesthood. When visiting my father in a nursing home during the last weeks of his life, I would see "Coach" laughing and talking cheerfully to both the residents and their attendants. He has a gift of making people smile and feel that they are important and loved. Coach is a mentor to me, someone who continues to work out a way to give others his time, his enthusiasm for life, his love. This kind of working out provides him with healthy life tones and flexibilities in his senior years.

> Life is short and we do not have much time to gladden the hearts of those who travel the way with us. So, be swift to love, make haste to be kind.
> —Henri Ariel

Decluttering

Most of us do not have large ears, big black eyes, and long tails like pack rats but some of us certainly have the same habits and behavioral patterns of these clutter-loving creatures.

Over the years many of us have accumulated, sometimes unwittingly, lots of stuff, boxes of framed pictures, old tax files, school report cards, beer coasters, all kinds of worn out old furniture. We have also accumulated truckloads of fears, anxieties, regrets, and resentments.

In a strange and ironic way, retirement is like a college commencement—a new beginning, an opportunity to "declutter" our life. It is a departure point—a time to leave behind much of our old "never worn" stuff. Someone once said that when we bring out our clothes for a new season, we should take to the Goodwill anything we haven't worn in the past year. Letting go of some of our old habits, patterns, and "stuff" may free us to explore new ways and untapped opportunities in our life.

And like some of our favorite clothes that have been packed away for months, in retirement we can unpack and refresh ideas that we previously did not have the time or energy to "wear" or pursue.

> Keep only those things that speak to your heart. Then take the plunge and discard all the rest. By doing this, you can reset your life and embark on a new lifestyle.
>
> —Marie Kondo

Silence and Solitude

It was a family vacation with three young children, tents, coolers, luggage, pop tarts in a small red station wagon that belched black diesel smoke as we chugged up the Rocky Mountain passes. Thank goodness we didn't have our family dog strapped on top of the car!

As we drove through the red desert sands of Arches National Park in Utah, I asked my wife to drive away for thirty minutes and leave me in the stillness of the desert. I climbed a rock and watched the most precious people in my life slowly disappear on the meandering road.

Sitting in silent solitude in the middle of the desert was a profoundly transformative experience. As I stared across the vast red sandstone rocks and arches and bright blue sky, there were no sounds except a high-pitched ringing in my ears. It was as if someone had punched my "pause button" and my life abruptly stood still—suspended in the moment on a big rock in the middle of the desert. My mind was swirling first with superficial thoughts but soon emotions seemed to rise like bubbles gurgling from a deep, thick viscous sea of the unconscious. I began to sense a powerful intimacy and connection with myself, with nature, with life, with God.

After a while I saw the little red station wagon winding its way back to me and when my family returned, I was filled with gratitude, joy, and love for them, for us, and for all of life.

God is the friend of silence. See how nature—trees, flowers, grass—grows in silence; see the stars, the moon and the sun, how they move in silence. . . . We need silence to be able to touch souls.

—Mother Teresa

Japanese Garden

When I retired, rather than a gold watch, my employer and friends gave me a rock wrapped in a box. After a few off-the-cuff wrong guesses, they told me they would help me create a Japanese rock garden at my home. In anticipation of retirement, I had decided not to find an office but convert a small bedroom into a study—a personal place to read, write, and reflect. One wall of my study is floor-to-ceiling glass with a sliding glass door opening into a small courtyard.

Their gift enabled me to work with Nick, a young botanist and gardener responsible for the largest Japanese garden in town. Nick, a former rugby player, is a mountain of a man with a thick beard, and tattoos running all the way down his muscular arms and legs. He seemed to always work with a lollipop in his mouth. We worked together on a design that would embody the traditions and culture of the "Zen" gardens in Japan. We decided to create a dry rock garden (*karesansui*) using white granite pebbles, large stones, dwarf azaleas, and mondo grass. We went together to a "rock farm" and selected three five-hundred-pound rocks, which were delivered to my street curb by a huge dump truck. We rented a large crane and lifted bags of dirt, the rocks, and pebbles over my eight-foot brick wall and carefully positioned them into a simple, minimalist design.

The white pebbles represent water. The rocks are arranged like small islands in harmony with each other. Water and stone are the yin and yang in Buddhist symbolism. Zen legend says that it is a good omen for the stream (white pebbles representing water) to arrive from the east and meander around the rocks (islands representing heaven, earth, and humanity) and then leave in the west; this water journey will carry away evil, and the owner of the garden will be healthy and have a long life.

As I write this reflection, I am sitting in my study watching the light and shadows shift and dance in the garden against the tall white brick wall. I am hopeful that the legend of the karesansui will apply to me, too. I never did want a gold watch.

In His Hands

Those who joyfully leave everything in God's hand
will see God's hand in everything.

—Nishan Panwar

Six months after the earthquake, I walked through the iron gate surrounded by a ten-foot concrete boundary wall topped with razor wire in Port-au-Prince, Haiti. Over 250,000 people had died in this devastating earthquake in January 2010. As part of an Episcopalian support team, I was visiting St. Vincent's Centre, an Episcopal school for handicapped children.

A middle-aged man with a big smile, no arms, and no legs was propped in a chair and welcomed us in perfect English. He had been a resident at St. Vincent's since he was a small child and had learned three languages and now was a well-known artist who painted with a brush held in his lips.

School was in session, with several classrooms filled with eager students—some blind, some deaf, some with missing limbs, but all focused and engaged in learning the material and from each other. Many sighted children waved to me with a winsome smile as I passed by their temporary plywood classrooms. The original buildings of the school had collapsed in the earthquake, killing seven children and teachers and severely injuring others.

In the distance, I heard a choir singing a somewhat familiar hymn. I climbed steps to a second-floor classroom and peered through an open window to see over a dozen teenagers led by an adult choirmaster. Everyone in the room was blind. They were joyfully singing in Creole—"li gen lemonn antye nan men men'l." Although I don't understand Creole, I knew the tune and could sing quietly to myself: He's got the whole world in his hands.

I remember that almost everyone had a beaming smile as they held hands and swayed with the music. It was a sacred moment to experience their special brew of joy, faith, hope, courage, and love all in their beautiful young voices and their innocent faces. I was humbled as I realized that God's hand and presence was in this poor devastated country, in this school, in the hearts of these children, and even in me.

Humility

For several years a small group of guys from across the country have gathered for a weekend in South Alabama to hunt turkeys on a beautiful longleaf pine plantation.

Sitting camouflaged in the woods is a thrilling place to watch the sunrise and hear awakening songs of the birds and the scurrying sounds of the wood creatures.

Turkey hunting requires considerable skill, patience, and a calm presence when the big "toms" come yelping.

We call ourselves the Cedar Plank Gang because the cabin is made from hand-hewn cedar. This is where I first met Jimmy. He was a small, humble man with a big heart.

Jimmy used to be a cook on an oil tanker steaming through the North Pacific Ocean. He retired early after being diagnosed with a progressive neurological muscular disorder. Even though he couldn't move around very well, he had an athletic mind with a sharp wit and a great sense of humor. Jimmy didn't really care much about shooting turkeys but enjoyed the camaraderie and fellowship of our gang. After a morning out in the woods, we would share stories of our hunting adventures. Jimmy was the "pot-stirrer" who kept everyone relaxed and laughing together. He was always thinking of others. He loved to serve us bowls of turkey gumbo, grill cedar-planked salmon, and warm up homemade blueberry pies.

Jimmy had a wonderful way of coupling his lively wit with his humility. His presence in the group provided a safe place to be authentic and intimate. This was truly a unique gift for a group of men to share with each other their innermost thoughts and feelings.

Jimmy died a few years ago. After his death, the Cedar Plank Gang has continued to gather annually at the cabin and share our stories. Jimmy's spirit is with us and often we find ourselves laughing with tears in our eyes. His wake of wit and humility will continue to ripple through our hearts.

> Humility is not thinking less of yourself, but thinking of yourself less.
>
> —C.S. Lewis

The Mirror

In the opening line of Shakespeare's Hamlet, Bernardo calls out, "Who is there?" Leaning against a bathroom sink with a light overhead, I look at myself in the mirror and ask, meekly, who is there? I am staring through a glass onto a shiny, silver backing that captures light and sends a reproduction back out through the glass.

Who is this later-aged man with a receding hairline, wire-rimmed glasses, and lined face? Who is the observer, observing himself? What are his thoughts, attitudes, beliefs? What is he made of? How does he function?

As I stare at this face, it begins to lose its familiarity. Little by little, each piece evolves subtly into an object—someone else's nose, mouth, eyes, and ears. There is no suggestion of time passing—no past or future. There is no hint of the depth of space, no signals of thoughts and feelings, of relationships. But, I am conscious, I am aware of this moment and I know in part whose I am.

In the book of Genesis it says that we are made in the image of God. We may realize that we are gazing upon our humanity and, at the same time, pondering the deep mystery of God.

> For now we see in a mirror, dimly, but then we will see face to face. Now I know only in part; then I will know fully, even as I have been fully known.
>
> —1 Corinthians 13:12

Life Cycles

"History doesn't repeat itself, it just rhymes" is a saying often attributed to Mark Twain. There are patterns in our life that are repeated (and sometimes rhyme) but have different meanings at different times in our journey.

The book of Ecclesiastes lays out the cyclical view: "To every thing there is a season, and a time to every purpose under the heaven: A time to be born, and a time to die, a time to plant, and a time to pluck up that which is planted" (3:1–2, KJV).

Our life flows through non-linear cycles of change and continuity. Basic life themes reappear but like colored threads woven in a tapestry, these themes have different meanings and are nuanced in new contexts. Life is a flow, a chaotic, unpredictable adventure into a future of stability and instability. Our challenge is to learn how to confront and respond, how to manage these flow shifts, these life transitions. Patterns in our lives may seem to rhyme or even be repeated, but our experiences in every present moment are unique and once in a lifetime.

> No man ever steps in the same river twice, for it's not the same river and he's not the same man. You could not step twice into the same rivers; for other waters are ever flowing on to you.
>
> —Heraclitus

The Snow Leopard

There were three men hiking in the mountains . . . a priest, a bishop, and a Zen Buddhist master. No, this is not the beginning of a joke. Actually, I was privileged to join this threesome trekking the Annapurna range in Nepal a few years ago. A guide and two sherpas accompanied us as we traversed switchbacks that meandered up the mountains, past several small villages nestled among the boulders and trees. Many of these Nepalese families were living off the grid using manual tools and water buffalo like their ancestors for centuries.

The trails were surrounded with giant rhododendrons laced with wild orchids and mountain flowers. These paths were easily marked, having been the primary routes over the Himalayas to Tibet for thousands of years. Most of the time, the skies were cloudy but every now and then the clouds would part revealing snow-capped peaks against a background of a crystal blue sky.

In the late afternoons, we would arrive at teahouses owned and run by an entire family. Before our usual dinner of *daal bhaat* (rice and lentils), homegrown vegetables, and *momos* (dumplings), I would slump down on a bench and read *The Snow Leopard* by Peter Matthieson. He came to realize that his adventurous quest through this same Annapurna range was not for a sighting of the snow leopard but for a deeper understanding of his own sense of being:

"The elusive animal, the elusive truth, is on our inner path. But, going to an unfamiliar place can jar our awareness, can break our encrusted construct of our self, and lead us into the unfamiliar and mysterious liminality of the sacred."

As the evenings faded into the cool starlit nights, my three companions and I would silently and humbly stare at the now darkened mountains. There was an unspoken, intimate, and reassuring sense of community. We felt "jarred" to a deeper place of being, closer to the "mysterious liminality of the sacred."

Planning for Change

When my grandson turned age five, I gave him a LEGO kit to build an airplane. I watched him quietly putting together pieces in a slow, careful, methodical process. He couldn't read well but the directions were all pictures and as long as he didn't take any short cuts, the airplane slowly began to appear from the mass of plastic pieces. Within an hour he proudly beamed his success and zoomed the airplane around the room, making predictable airplane buzzing sounds.

We all know that our life cannot be put together with a simple, step-by-step manual like the LEGO puzzle! Of course we need plans and strategies to prepare for retirement, to anticipate our financial needs, unexpected emergencies, and place to live. How many of our plans turn out the way we thought? Think about how many of our major life events—relationships, homes, jobs—just appeared out of the blue. Many of our plans are quickly dismantled when external events and forces intervene.

Life is not rolled out from a well-conceived plan or playbook but is more of a journey of becoming. We are continually challenged to adapt and respond to changes. In our imaginary kayak, we have to be vigilant and guide our way in, around, and through the changes in our life.

There is no rushing a river. When you go there, you go at the pace of the water and that pace ties you into a flow that is older than life on this planet. Acceptance of that pace, even for a day, changes us, reminds us of other rhythms beyond the sound of our own heartbeats.

—Jeff Rennicke

Some People's Special Ways

Jerry is younger. On some Saturdays, he helps me in my yard doing the heavy lifting and strenuous digging and climbing ladders. (One of the cardinal rules in retirement is never climb a ladder!) He has good common sense and is "street wise." One early morning we were driving through my neighborhood to my home. There was a man dusting his roses in one yard. He was someone I had known since childhood and I have always thought he was little "off" and a bit odd. I casually remarked to Jerry that this man was really weird. Jerry smiled and quietly said: " Now, some peoples have their ways and some peoples have their special ways."

That was a lesson in humility! We all are sometimes quick to judge others. Strangely, we all have our "special" ways and should be more attentive and understanding of others.

> You never really understand a person until you consider things from his point of view [. . .] until you climb into his skin and walk around in it.
>
> —Harper Lee, *To Kill a Mockingbird*

Rip Currents

A rip current is a strong, localized current of water that moves directly away from the shore, cutting through the lines of breaking waves. The location of rip currents can be unpredictable: while some tend to recur always in the same place, others can appear and disappear suddenly at various locations along the shore.

When caught in a rip current, it is advisable to just relax, if you can, swim laterally and don't fight the strong current. At first you will be swept away from shore but eventually the current will die out and then you can swim back to the beach and to safety.

Most of us have been caught in rip currents in our lives. One moment for me was the day my mother died. I thought I was prepared for her death—she had been seriously ill and bedridden for years. When I was told she had died, my heart sank deep into my chest.

It was a cold, gray January day. I went for a run across a golf course with a fierce winter wind blowing in my face. I remember muttering, "Mother, I love you, I miss you!" I was caught in a powerful emotional riptide—a swirling of intense feelings of sadness, loss, home-sickness, and even self-pity. I couldn't think straight so I just ran harder into the headwinds.

It took some time with family and friends before I could return to "shore" and resume my life with this new and radically different identity as a motherless child.

Time is a sort of river of passing events, and strong is its current; no sooner is a thing brought to sight than it is swept by and another takes its place, and this too will be swept away.

—Marcus Aurelius

Restreaming

Fully Alive

Little goldfish swimming in a round glass bowl really don't have many options in their daily life patterns. Most goldfish are seen to be in a predictable pattern of eating, sleeping, pooping, and swimming around the bowl time after time. But some goldfish, I would like to imagine, have an incredibly optimistic outlook as they peer through the fish bowl. Every time around they seem to exclaim: "Wow! Look at that!" and again: "Wow! Look at that!"

Studies have shown that a key to good health is to hold on to positive thoughts. Having a positive outlook about the world and even the future will enrich and nourish life. Daily patterns and predictable routines provide a healthy sense of rhythm in our life. Maintaining our routines reduces stress in our bodies and keeps us comfortable and in a balanced, homeostatic state of being. But . . . every now and then, we need to be awakened, startled, and even challenged to break away from predictability and view the world with fresh eyes and hope. We should welcome and be receptive to our condition of amazement. When Moses saw God's glory in the burning bush; when Ezekial saw the glory; when the women discovered the tomb was empty, when I watched my daughter giving birth to my grandson: Wow, look at that!

The Glory of God is a human being fully alive.

—St. Iraneaus

Pursuing Unanswerable Questions

On her deathbed, Gertrude Stein is said to have asked, "What is the answer?" Then, after a long silence, "What is the question?"

Questions are not just random thoughts but lead us sometimes to the needs of our deepest self—they are our spiritual teachings. Uncertainty is implicit in the human condition. We can find answers to simple questions and even complex ones when relying on academic skill sets like mathematics, statistics, geology, physics, and others. But, what are the answers to the deeper meaning-filled questions, the ones that pique our interest in our beginnings, our identities, our destinies?

Dr. Rachel Remen, a physician and author, once wrote that her aim in life is to pursue unanswerable questions in good company. In a loose paraphrase of her "aim in life," we are drawn to pursue the mysteries of the Universe (God) with people in meaningful relationships. We follow the paths of others in our humble, meager, yet collegial quest for meaning. In pursuing unanswerable questions, we can become aware that being in relationships with others on the journey may lead us to the answers.

Be patient toward all that is
unsolved in our heart and
try to love the questions
themselves ... live everything.
Live the questions now.

—Rainer Maria Rilke

If Not Now, Then When?

There is an old adage that bad news doesn't improve with age. Studies indicate that 20 percent of the adult population is made up of chronic procrastinators.

There are times in our life when we dodge the difficult issues, postpone things that are uncomfortable, avoid confrontations with difficult people. Procrastination can create dangerously high levels of stress, causing sleepless nights and placing us at risk for poor health. Habitual procrastinators are likely to avoid seeking treatments for medical problems.

Sometimes procrastinating is necessary to sort out a complex task or relationship. A deliberate delay may help calm initial emotions so that responses are more measured and appropriate. We may even realize that certain projects, tasks, or relationships are not worth pursuing. Perhaps it would be worthwhile to create a "not to do list" as well as a "to do" list.

In Stephen Covey's time management grid, we find ourselves frequently engaged and distracted in the third and fourth quadrants of "urgent and not important" and "not urgent and not important" areas.

Quadrant I: Urgent & Important	Quadrant II: Not Urgent & Important
Quadrant III: Urgent & Not Important	Quadrant IV: Not Urgent & Not Important

Stephen Covey's Time Management Grid, US Geological Survey, Department of Employee and Organizational Development, https://www2.usgs.gov/humancapital/documents/TimeManagementGrid.pdf (accessed April 3, 2017).

When we are drawn into the busyness of immediate tasks, we may discover that we have not allowed ourselves enough time to engage in the second quadrant of "important and not urgent" times in our life. This is the area that provides us with the opportunity to explore new insights, discover meaningful relationships, and create new visions and plans for our future. This "important and not urgent" area is a place where our physical health and spiritual growth can be nurtured and our lives enriched.

Legacy

In 1952 Kemmons Wilson took his wife and five children on a road trip to Washington, D.C. He was disappointed with the quality of the motels along the way. A few months later he opened the first Holiday Inn and in 1972, with over 1,400 Holiday Inns throughout the country, Mr. Wilson was on the cover of *Time* magazine. I know his sons and daughters and occasionally would see him around town. A few years ago I was walking through a new Holiday Inn planning an upcoming convention with the hotel events coordinator. She suggested that we visit the mezzanine level that displayed all of Mr. Wilson's memorabilia and awards. The walls were thick with pictures of Mr. Wilson with presidents, celebrities, kings, queens, and various awards from around the world.

In the middle of the room there was a man in a wheelchair with a caretaker. I recognized it as Mr. Wilson and introduced myself. We had a pleasant and brief conversation about his distinguished achievements and awards. I casually mentioned that he must feel proud and pleased of all he had accomplished over the span of his life. He furrowed his brow and muttered that all of this stuff is not really important to him anymore. He then looked up at me with a peaceful smile and said: "What has been most important to me is that I have been blessed with the love of my family, my dear friends, and my faith in God."

Mr. Wilson dedicated his life to building a hotel empire while at the same time he and his wife raised a family of five children with love and devotion for each other and the world around them.

A common perception is to think about a legacy as tied to a financial inheritance. Recent studies however indicate that today's retirees are two times more likely to perceive their legacy in their capacity to pass on values and life lessons rather than financial assets. Perhaps even more surprisingly, younger generations agree with their priority of values and life lessons.

Mr. Wilson, in my eyes, was a great man who was blessed with a full life, knowing his priorities and living into them every step of the way. His five children and their children have carried on his legacy.

Mountain Tops

A common metaphor for pursuing goals is climbing mountains. Each step along the way is to be savored, not just a means to an end but a unique event in itself.

Robert Persig wrote in his classic book *Zen and the Art of Motorcycle Maintenance*, "To live only for some future goal is shallow. It's the sides of the mountains which sustain life, not the top. Here's where things grow. But, of course, without the top, you can't have any sides. It's the top that defines the sides."

In our later years, we discover new dreams, set new goals, and start our pursuit with patient awareness of all that is growing around us. With each step, we will have the opportunity to engage in life. We become fully present with whatever comes our way. We will climb based on our abilities and desires.

We may never reach our goal, our mountaintop, yet we can experience simple pleasures, companionship, and pursuit of causes beyond ourselves. We can begin to understand a subtle shift from a life based on ambition and achievement to a life based on our legacy—what we have to give back to others. It's these moments that enrich our lives, where things grow and can even become our personal mountain-top experiences.

It is good to have an end to journey towards; but it is the journey that matters in the end.

—Ursula K. LeGuin

Randomness and Patterns of Life

On the weekend of April 2, 2015, my wife and I were on our way to a wedding in Virginia and took a side trip to Appomattox. This was the weekend before the 150th anniversary of Confederate general Robert E. Lee's surrender to Lieutenant General Ulysses S. Grant.

We walked through the meadows, reading about the placement of the regiments as they braced for battle. There were a few cannons but no sign of blue or grey coats lurking in the surrounding woods. As we were leaving, my wife asked the ranger if there were records to establish the presence of her great-grandfather. She had heard the family stories about his last assignment as a soldier in the Alabama infantry and walking back to Montgomery after the surrender. The ranger pulled out a thick book and after a lot of page-thumbing found him. The ranger pointed out the window and said that her great-grandfather spent the evening of April 8, 1865, on that knoll prior to Lee's surrender the next day.

I then asked about my great-grandfather, who had fought at Antietam, Gettysburg, and presumably was also with Lee at Appomattox. After flipping through another thick book he told us that my great-grandfather was with another regiment 1,500 yards north.

As we drove away from this ghostly experience, my wife and I were awed by the randomness and the patterns of it all. Somehow our great-grandfathers survived the Civil War and on that evening were within shouting distance. Their genes are now within our children and grandchildren.

Our journeys through life are riddled with randomness and happenstance. We seem to be thrown together in this strange world by twists of fate, jostled on our journeys like kayaks shifting constantly in the chaotic currents of an aggressive river. Yet we can also look back at our lives as orderly linear paths in the providential hands of God.

Everything we care about lies somewhere in the middle, where pattern and randomness interlace.

—James Gleick

Unity

There is a small Episcopal church in South Alabama, actually a modified double-wide trailer with a low-ceiled addition, hard wooden pews, and fluorescent lighting in the ceiling. I had decided to go there on a Sunday while on spring vacation and was greeted at the door with a firm handshake from a small smiling man wearing a red polo shirt with the big A for Alabama football on his front pocket.

There were about twenty people in the nave. The choir of six singers was accompanied by a trombone, a flute, and a plunky piano. Everyone was a little bit out of tune—especially the trombone player.

The priest was a woman I had known from many years ago. Before becoming a priest, she had lived on my street in Memphis. (Randomness or patterns in our lives?) She led the congregation with a dignified and authentic presence. After a short, provocative homily, we all participated in the Prayers of the People, a series of prayers that form part of the liturgy every Sunday in the Anglican, Roman Catholic, Lutheran, Methodist, and other Western liturgical churches.

I settled into the beauty and rhythm of this liturgy and thought about the thousands and thousands of people around the world who were reading the same scriptures and praying these same prayers. In this small, humble community, I sensed that we were all united and immersed in a holy Cloud of Unknowing, a palpable presence of God.

As we walked towards a simple wooden communion rail in front of the pews, I glanced through a clear glass window behind the altar and saw a dogwood tree in full bloom with delicate, white flowers. I realized then that everyone in that little church in South Alabama was, in the moment, a small, extraordinary piece of his creation.

> For in the one Spirit we were all baptized into one body—Jews or Greeks, slaves or free—and we were all made to drink of one Spirit.
>
> —1 Corinthians 12:13

Life Mastery Seminar

Several years ago I attended an executive MBA seminar session titled Life Mastery. As the class gathered, the facilitator passed out two sheets of paper to each of us. He asked us to sit quietly for five minutes and then write down quickly the three most important things in our lives and share our answers with the stranger sitting next to us. I jotted down a predictable list of God, Family, and Health.

After a few minutes the facilitator asked us to take the second sheet of paper and list three behaviors that consistently support and are aligned with our three important "things" and also list three behaviors that are inconsistent and/or detract us from them. I was astonished and somewhat uncomfortable to expose to the stranger and to myself with these lists and behaviors. This one-hour seminar has continued to provoke and haunt me. Now as I have restreamed, the open-ended questions are ringing even more truly and loudly.

> If you want to know me, don't ask where I live, what I like to eat, how I part my hair; rather, ask me what I live for, in every detail, and ask me what in my view prevents me from living fully for the thing I really want to live for.
>
> —Thomas Merton

Aged Out

Occasionally, I do some serious porch sitting with a handful of guys in rocking chairs, trying to solve the world's problems. There is one fellow in this group, Frankie (not his real name), who has the talent of capturing the essence of life's truths in short, accessible, and searingly honest phrases. He is truly a country philosopher with a repertoire of pithy and humorous aphorisms that set the whole gang of us in laughter and then in quiet reflection.

Frankie is one of those special men who gets up early every day and, as he says, "takes a mighty swing at the ball." Sometimes he connects, sometimes he misses, and sometimes he knocks a home run! What's important to him is making sure to take that swing—to be engaged in life whatever is thrown his way.

One afternoon Frankie was talking about grandchildren and their insatiable zeal to play in the water. Rocking in his chair with his bare foot on the back of my old yellow lab, he said that he had "aged out" of water sports. I began to think about what I had "aged out" of, including arduous hikes, baby strollers, heavy lifting, tall ladders, noisy restaurants, late-night movies, and the list went on and on. So, as I have aged out of these in my senior years, I began to realize I had aged into more reflection time, walks with my wife, grandchildren's soccer games, more doctors' visits, adult children, stronger coffee in the morning, good times with old friends, and more.

We would be well served to be attentive, aware, and live into the ways we have changed. We cannot be stagnant and stale in the rut of past successes. We can prepare ourselves to "take a swing" every day and "age into" a transformative life of adapting our physical, spiritual, and emotional self to the world around us.

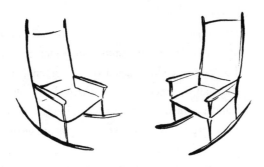

The only way to make sense out
of change is to plunge into it,
move with it, and join the dance.

—Alan Watts

Guns to Sailboats

For over fifty years I enjoyed duck hunting with my father and close friends deep in flooded hardwood timber in Mississippi. Standing in two to three feet of water behind trees, we would watch the daybreak and the wildlife come alive. I never really enjoyed shooting the ducks but loved every minute of just being in the middle of the woods experiencing a majestic sunrise and the unfolding of God's creation.

On December 14, 2012, in Newtown, Connecticut, twenty-year-old Adam Lanza walked into Sandy Hook Elementary School and fatally shot twenty children aged six and seven years old, as well as six adult staff members. After this tragedy, I really felt sad, disheartened, and ashamed of our country and the irrational zeal of many people to protect and preserve their rights under the Second Amendment of our Constitution.

I also was keenly aware that I had several shotguns in my home that could be a potential danger for me and my family.

In honest conversations with my wife and family, I decided painfully but not reluctantly to get rid of my shotguns and stop hunting ducks. At the time I didn't realize how this decision was a major shift in my life pattern. From Thanksgiving through the end of the year I had been hunting almost every weekend. I missed those early mornings in the woods.

I found a gun dealer in Florida and took my guns to FedEx to ship them away. When I placed them on the conveyor, I laid my hands on them one more time and appreciated their presence with me all of those years.

With the money from the sale of the guns, I was able to buy a little sailboat for my grandchildren. Although they will probably never experience a winter sunrise deep in the flooded woods calling ducks, I am pleased and relieved that they will be sailors and riding with the wind sometimes in the early morning as the sun is slowly rising over the water.

> . . . they will beat their swords into plowshares, and their spears into pruning hooks; nation shall not lift up sword against nation, neither shall they learn war any more.
>
> —Isaiah 2:4b

Gardening

Nikos Kazantzakis, in his book, *Report to Greco*, about St. Frances, writes: "I said to the almond tree, 'Sister, speak to me of God.' And the almond tree blossomed."

When we moved six years ago, we cut down scraggly hackberries, privet hedges, and other unsightly bushes and trees in the backyard. We planned a low-maintenance, "easy on the eyes," natural landscape with a variety of colors, shapes, and textures. Some plants were "allowed" to remain and we even transplanted (for the third time) my mother's quince—now over fifty years old.

Working in the soil with early morning rays warming my back, I have enjoyed the quiet, serene moments to pull weeds, water, and fertilize, taking time to appreciate the surrounding beauty of nature. Sometimes I just lie down on my back and watch the clouds drifting above and smell the fragrant earth. The garden is where growing happens. The trees and perennials planted six years ago have matured, and the colors of the seasons enthusiastically express the inherent glories of God's creation.

Our retirement transition can be viewed as a garden with an opportunity to remove some of the past, regrettable habits and ways of being. Both soil and soul need to be loosened up to allow growth. We can preserve some past important relationships and experiences and also pursue new ideas, new habits, and new friends, watching them grow into rich, integrated parts of our life.

There is a latent seed of wholeness in everyone and everything. We thrive when we take the time to water, fertilize, and nurture it. We thrive when we love it.

> We have the world to live in on the condition that we will take good care of it. And to take good care of it, we have to know it. And to know it and to be willing to take care of it, we have to love it.
>
> —Wendell Berry

The Process

Some friends are frankly astonished when they discover my tribal zeal for the Alabama Crimson Tide. After all, it's been forty-nine years since I left the campus, and I have only attended two games—both in the past five years. Allowing time for Saturday afternoon SEC football, however, is relaxing and uplifting fun—especially when my tribe is winning!

The current coach, Nick Saban, has crafted winning teams through a strategy he calls "the process." His way of doing things is very methodical and focused, with keen attention to the details. It is all about doing what you can control, every minute of every day. Each player learns specific techniques and assignments in blocking, tackling, running, and passing. Attention to the little things each day can make great things happen. The bigger picture isn't the focus, but all those little steps taken that filled it out.

Retirement can be viewed as a "process." We are in the inevitable process of aging and challenged to pay attention to the "little things" and the little steps that fill out our lives. Ram Dass, the American spiritual author, suggests that life is the ultimate spiritual teacher, we cannot learn unless we attend school. We are challenged to be in the present and to participate in the process of life. We learn by experience and a process of taking one step at a time.

Mrs. Massey

On Tuesday mornings, I call Mrs. Massey when I am three blocks away . . . "Good morning Mrs. Massey, this is Tuesday Bill about to reach your doorstep with a hot meal."

Since my retirement, I volunteer weekly to deliver hot meals to men and women who are frail, elderly, alone, and cannot cook for themselves. There are twenty stops on my route in South Memphis and Mrs. Massey is my favorite. She has had knee and hip replacements and now slowly gets around on a walker. Her door is double locked for security in her rundown neighborhood where she has lived for over fifty years.

When she finally opens the door, we both break into broad smiles. She calls me Tuesday Bill since I see her every Tuesday morning. We talk briefly about her past week's experiences and the joy of living another day by the grace of God. Sometimes I wonder if I am her only connection with the outside world all day. As I leave, I bend over and peck her cheek lightly. She always says goodbye with a warm thanks and a soft murmuring prayer . . . "Tuesday Bill, be careful and know that God loves you."

The image of her smile stays with me as I move on to my next "Meals on Wheels" stop.

Memory

> Life can only be understood backwards; but it must be lived forwards.
>
> —Søren Kierkegaard

The stroke of the paddle creates a whirl of ripples that are left behind the kayak and slowly ease out until they either dissipate or roll up on the riverbank. Once the kayak has glided downstream, there are no traces of its ever being on the river. The only thing that continues to "exist" of that moment is lodged in the memory of the kayaker with the capacity to see the past.

As we look back on our experiences, we can only approximate what happened in our lives. Our minds can be triggered by old photographs, returning to places where something happened, listening to others who may have shared the same experiences.

Even though we cannot return to the past physically, our memories and our learnings from experiences can continue to "live" on, providing us with insight, perspective, and wisdom. We could call these collective memories our spirits of the past. With every stroke of our paddle, with every moment of our life, we are given the opportunity to learn something and guide us along the way.

First Love

When I think about my first love, I skip right over my teenage years and early girlfriend experiences and settle back in my memories as a young child at my grandparents' house. Their bedroom was a row of iron beds on a sleeping porch with lots of windows. On hot summer nights, a black rotating Emerson fan cooled the still air with a gentle breeze. We called my grandmother Mamie. She had the softest hands and would rub our backs, singing lullabies that she had heard as a little child. In these sleepy moments, I felt the warmth and strength of her love. She enjoyed quoting Bible verses, poems, and nursery rhymes. One that I still remember well was:

The three were walking on a wall,
Feeling, Faith, and Love,
When Feeling took an awful fall
And Faith was tottering above
So close was Faith to Feeling
That Faith stumbled and fell too
But Love remained and
Pulled Faith back
And Faith brought Feeling too.

Love is like that, I guess, strong, ubiquitous, and can be called upon when things are going the wrong way. As I read Paul's letter to the Corinthians about love, I think of Mamie and her enduring and gentle love for me and for everyone she knew.

Seeking Wisdom

One of my most admired and respected mentors was an older friend named Bob. He was a true renaissance man—a priest, historian, psychologist, author, teacher, father, and grandfather. He was humble, self-effacing, and could listen closely to others' stories with his mind and his heart. Bob and I met for breakfast almost every month for years. I cherished those times to "sit at his feet" and query him about life. He would share books and poems and we would dive into deep conversations about existentialism, theological proclivities, and spiritual well-being. We didn't solve many problems but we became aware of how much we did not know.

As I reflect on our relationship, I am surprised that Bob really never gave me advice. He just had a special way of listening and reframing questions. It was almost as if we were dancing with each other in a spiritual, metaphorical way. He would lead and I would respond, he would lift up an idea, and I would inflate it with more ideas. Bob was a sower of wisdom, inviting me to plant seeds of wisdom through reflection, imitation, and experience.

Confucius wrote that there are three ways to learn wisdom: first, by reflection, which is noblest; second, by imitation, which is easiest; and third by experience, which is the bitterest.

In our later years, we become more aware that our time on this earth is limited. We are much further downstream in our life. Time seems to be quickening. Our priorities and interests have shifted. We no longer pursue the "achievement tributaries." There is little or no interest to prove ourselves. Our focus is more on family and old, established friends. We understand more fully the importance of being rather than just doing.

As we ease into this subtle life-changing shift, we sense a sober, deeper understanding of our place on this earth. We may even begin to appreciate the emerging importance of seeking wisdom in our lives.

In our long life of reflections, relationships, and experiences, we learn to see not by looking but by understanding the deeper essence of our self.

> God grant me the serenity to accept the things I cannot change, the courage to change the things I can, and the wisdom to know the difference.
>
> —Reinhold Niebuhr

Down Times

Sometimes on our journey in our imaginary kayak, we become weary with it all. The days may run together with no spark, no joy, no wonder. It is in these down times that we need to fall back into our habits, settle into daily routines, and allow ourselves to relax and be more aware of the unseen currents carrying us along.

Simone Weil writes about being attentive, allowing ourselves to wait "not seeking anything but ready to receive." This attention, this awareness could be the same thing as prayer. Think of the parable, she says. Attention is the lamp filled with oil awaiting the bridegroom's coming. And what if he's late and our lamps burn out? There's oil in the jar, there at our side, hidden away for the day it's needed. We have filled that jar just for this moment. We wait with attention and patience.

The current underneath continues to carry us further on our journey even in our down times. And with patience and time, we are engaged again in sparks of new life, joy, and wonder.

> You may encounter many defeats, but you must not be defeated. In fact, it may be necessary to encounter the defeats, so you can know who you are, what you can rise from, how you can still come out of it.
>
> —Maya Angelou

La Baguette Brothers

The coffee is too weak for my taste and the cinnamon rolls too sweet, but I still go to the La Baguette pastry shop on Thursday mornings at 7:30 am. For the past twenty years a small group of men from my church gather together informally in the back room of the store to read the gospel lesson for the upcoming Sunday. For the next hour, we share stories, anecdotes, metaphors, and even jokes, straying and then coming back to the selected Scripture. Our approach to the lessons is informal, personal, and insightful.

Over the years we have become a band of brothers with a deeply held earned intimacy and authenticity. Some weeks the Scripture seems to resonate with our own lives, other times we are engaged in shared stories of our joys, pains, fears, and complexities. For many of us, this hour together is really a sacred, cherished, and God-inspired time. We close the session by holding hands and offering prayers for each other and for those who are in trouble, sorrow, sickness, need, or any other kind of adversity. The coffee is always a little weak but our relationships are always strong.

> For where two or three are gathered in my name, I am there among them.
>
> —Matthew 18:20

Pilgrim People

We sometimes reach a stage in life when we wish we could nestle down in a comfortable wayside shelter. We want to just stop and stay there for good, to give up the journey. But that is to deny or forget our Abramic roots—pitching tents and moving on.

Just as ships are not built to rest safely in harbors, we are created to journey out into the open seas—to engage in life with vigor and astonishment. Life is not a spectator sport but an adventure, an experience where you don't know how it will turn out.

In the eleventh century, St. Bernard wrote that people journey to God not by the steps of their feet but by the turning of their hearts. May Sarton reminds us that our pilgrimage toward our true self will take time, many years and many places. We will need patience, courage, and passion to make the journey for our own sake and for the sake of others. But we must push forward.

We are a pilgrim people—we need to get back in our kayak, push away from the comfortable, wayside eddy and move on downstream. The future will be unclear, foggy. In this each of us must find his or her own way until our life stream pours into God's ocean of eternal love.

The motto on Jacques Cousteau's ship, the Calypso, was *Il faut aller voir*—"We must go and see for ourselves."

Play

How often do we feel the freedom of not needing to take our plans, our thoughts, ourselves too seriously? Taking a break from life's distractions and complications can be restorative and life-giving.

While I was having lunch with two good friends one day recently, they asked if I wanted to go "birding." Frankly, in the past I thought it a bit odd to spend a day with binoculars, cameras, and bird books looking through the trees for elusive feathered things. But I enjoy being with good friends and decided to take them up on a bird outing.

We went to a state park and drove slowly through the woods. Unfortunately the foliage was thick and most of the birds, they said, were hidden behind the leaves and bushes. Suddenly, two beautiful little birds with brilliant blue plumage flew swiftly in front of the car and landed on a branch by the road. My friend identified them as indigo buntings and explained their habitats and habits. I tried to control my enthusiasm but was really just chirping like a bird with excitement. Later we sighted a great blue heron, red-winged blackbirds, and a pileated woodpecker. The day was filled with surprises, delightful company, and healthy fellowships.

> We don't stop playing because we grow old; we grow old because we stop playing.
>
> —George Bernard Shaw

Hope vs. Optimism

Optimism is going after Moby Dick in a rowboat and taking the tartar sauce with you. This is a rough translation of a Zig Ziglar aphorism, substituting the word "confidence" with "optimism." Optimism is the belief that things are going to get better, we just need to wait and see. It's a passive position that underestimates risks and disregards or ignores the challenges of reality. A positive attitude towards life is important and breeds a sense of well-being but it must be embedded in hope, not blind optimism.

Vaclav Havel, the great Czech writer, philosopher, and statesman, writes of hope as a state of mind, a dimension of the soul. It is not dependent on our observation of the world or an estimate of a situation. It transcends the world and is anchored somewhere beyond its horizons. Hope is not the conviction that something will turn out well (Moby Dick and tartar sauce). Hope is the certainty that something makes sense, regardless of how it turns out. Hope gives us the strength to live, meeting the challenges in our lives with conviction that there is meaning and purpose in what we do, how we respond.

George, a good friend in the Thursday morning Bible group, has late-stage pancreatic cancer with only weeks to live. In conversations with him, he does not glibly say with superficial optimism that things will get better soon. He confronts reality and is keenly aware that his days are limited. He has a deep feeling of hope that his life has been lived with integrity and that he has been surrounded with love from his family, his friends, and his God. He has not lost hope.

> The best and most beautiful things in the world cannot be seen or even touched—they must be felt with the heart.
>
> —Helen Keller

The Good Man

There was an old, good man walking alone in the woods when God came down out of the clouds and spoke to him, saying, "Good man, you have lived and loved well, I will grant you any wish." The good man quietly wished that he could make a positive difference in other people's lives. God spoke to him again, saying, "Good man, your wish is granted."

Good man smiled and walked further into the woods and suddenly stopped and prayed to God for another wish. God came down out of the clouds again and spoke to him, saying, "Good man, you have lived long and loved well, I will grant you a second wish." The good man quietly wished not only that he could make a positive difference in other people's lives but that they would not know it was him that made the difference. God spoke to him again, saying, "Good man, your second wish is granted."

Good man smiled and walked even further into the woods and suddenly stopped and prayed to God for a third wish. God came down out of the clouds again and, in his infinite patience, spoke to him again, saying, "Good man, you have lived long and loved well, I will grant you a third wish." The good man humbly wished not only that he could make a positive difference in other people's lives, and not only that they would not know it was him that made the difference, but that he would not even know that he was making a difference in their lives. God spoke to him a third time and said that all three wishes will be granted and was deeply pleased that the good man had loved well from his heart.

Perhaps the purest form of love is one that gives and gives, does not count the cost, and is simply not even aware of the love gift. In our later years, we are positioned and privileged in life to be generative, giving of ourselves to others without expecting anything in return.

John

John and I were childhood friends. We grew up together and shared adolescent and adult experiences. We did things we should have regretted and things that we wouldn't dare tell anyone! He was gifted with a sharp intellect, good looks, and an enthusiasm for life. His early years attending a fundamentalist congregation drove him away from traditional religion. I knew him as someone who would not darken the doors of a church, but was spiritual, with a deep compassion for others.

In the prime of his life, he was diagnosed with cancer and given a few years to live. He continued his career as an architect for longer than expected but seemed to focus more and more on the open-ended questions of what makes a life meaningful and the unknowable nature of death. We would stay up late at night talking about how our lives had unfolded and to what end we were placed on this earth.

In the weeks prior to his death, John was riddled with pain and heavily medicated. He was conscious and occasionally had that engaging smile for me when I walked into his room. On one of my last visits, he wanted to take a shower one more time. I borrowed one of his bathing suits and with the help of his wife, walked him slowly to the shower. He was hooked up to an IV and other medical supports. We stood under the warm shower together and began to laugh and cry at the same time. In a way, the water was a baptism, cleansing not only his worn-out body but his mind and soul as he prepared to die. After the shower, he asked me to lie down by his side, hold his hand, and repeat the twenty-third Psalm while he listened with his eyes closed.

John died soon after that visit and I continue to be challenged by his spirit and zealous pursuit for meaning in life.

> Challenging the meaning of life is the truest expression of the state of being human.
>
> —Viktor E. Frankl

Geezers to Classics

On Saturday mornings at 7:15 sharp, six of us meet at the park to run three or four miles together. With an average age well north of seventy, we really don't run but slow jog (slog) together, catching up on movies, politics, books, and health issues. At younger ages, we were all running addicts with over fifty marathons collectively among us. (I never knew whether I was running to get away or to chase my ideas and dreams.)

We used to call ourselves the Geezers but that label didn't wear well. We now are called the Classics—much more respectable and dignified. We celebrate our birthdays with pancake breakfasts after our runs and once a year take a weekend trip together to run, relax, grill, tell stories, and laugh together. A recent trip was to Kiawah Island, and we ran early in the morning, barefooted, along a flat beach in the receding tide and felt like we were young again as we hummed "Chariots of Fire."

> For decades we ran
> Together silently
> Learning each other's pace
> And now on this beach
> Our bare feet slapping the shallow pools
> We rhythmically moved
> Toward another sunrise, another day
> A loose-knit brotherhood
> Bound together with unspoken joy and gratitude.

Walking with Wisdom

Almost every week I visit my aunt, my father's younger sister. At age ninety-four and wheelchair-bound, she remains enthusiastic and hopeful about life and possesses an insatiable curiosity. Our afternoon talks seem to always begin with her question: "Well, what's been going on with you and the family?" As I share with her recent events she has a subtle and wise way of knowing what is important and meaning-making in my weekly activities.

I have known her my whole life and have always admired her intelligence, her faith, and her compassion for others. She has walked with deep faith through the loss of two husbands, the closing of her beloved church, and serious illnesses and has somehow integrated these experiences into a coherent wholeness and an indomitable love that embraces everyone she meets along the way.

It is probably true that we learn to walk by falling down. I am keenly aware that my aunt has time and time again fallen and then stood back up and continued "walking" with an integrity of love. She has a wisdom way of walking as a loving companion with her nephew on an open-ended and evolving spiritual path. I have indeed been privileged to be with her, soaking up as much wisdom as possible on these sacred talks and walks.

Controlling Direction and Speed

Imagine we are in our kayak with our double-bladed paddle as our only tool to control direction and speed. So, let's allow our imagination to float along in this current (remember, we are now going downstream!). In the rhythm of our daily life, what areas can we control? Diet? Exercise? Relationships? Behaviors? Purpose?

We all have a passion for control but are also aware that we cannot control the uncontrollable. There are external forces that may abruptly impact us like a meteor slamming the earth's crust or a cancer diagnosis that suddenly becomes real. If some things are uncontrollable, why are we then worried about them? Can we avoid those areas that we cannot control? In anticipation of possible "white-water rapids" around the bend, can we paddle to safety or at least avoid the most treacherous rocks in our lives? How well do we adjust and adapt to external forces? Two millennia ago, Marcus Aurelius reminded us that it's not our experiences that form us but the ways in which we respond to them. We can learn to control our responses even to the uninvited forces that bear upon us.

In retirement, we can find the time and the practices that become habits to learn to be intentional, disciplined, and to aggressively direct our relationships, diet, exercise (both physical and spiritual), and the pursuit of our life's aim or purpose.

Studies have shown that having a sense of control can make a positive impact on our health and well-being. And, we also must have the sense to recognize that while there are forces in our life that we cannot control, we can always control our responses.

> I can't change the direction of the wind, but I can adjust my sails to always reach my destination.
>
> —Jimmy Dean

Gratitude

My wife, sister, and stepmother walked into the rehab center to share with my father the news that he would be going to a nursing home to live out his days. We were all uneasy and unsure how he would react to this radical move. He was ninety-three years old and had suffered a debilitating stroke a year earlier.

My father, in his twenties, was a World War II bomber pilot with over fifty missions and a recipient of many distinguished medals and honors. His postwar life was shaped by this formative experience. He was very competitive, a strong leader in the community, and enjoyed a high-profile life of recognition and achievement. He had outlived my mother, almost all of his friends and contemporaries, and had remarried at age seventy-eight. After visiting close friends in nursing homes over the years, he had frequently remarked that he hoped that he would never have to be placed into one.

When we walked into his room and told him that we had secured a place for him at the neighborhood nursing home, he smiled with tears in his eyes and said that he was deeply thankful. For the next six months, until he succumbed to his illnesses, he was filled with gratitude for the love of his family. My daughters and grandchildren frequently visited him and he seemed to "rise to the occasion" and was grateful for their compassion and love.

Gratitude came late for my father, but his last days were special times of thankfulness and heartfelt acceptance of others' love for him.

> If the only prayer you ever say in your entire life is thank you, it will be enough.
>
> —Meister Eckart

Being Withness

Dr. René Descartes was sitting at a bar, drinking the last drops of his glass of whisky. The bartender walked over and said, "Dr. Descartes, would you like another shot of whisky?" Dr. Descartes exclaimed, "I think not." And suddenly, he disappeared!

Perhaps his life didn't happen that way but the story certainly aligns with his famous phrase, "*Cogito ergo sum*," I think, therefore I am. Comparing being with identity is not only complex but also dangerously egotistical and unhealthy. This line of thinking, this intellectual ontology, has greatly influenced our modern framework of self—drawing us into a smaller sense of ourselves. Loneliness is toxic.

Recent studies have consistently identified that the single most important indicator of our happiness and sense of well-being is our relationships with others. The classic Harvard study of 724 men begun in 1938 and tracking them over seventy-five years concluded that good relationships keep us healthy, happy, and living longer.

Martin Buber articulated this critical relational ontology with his famous work *I and Thou*, but the idea goes back much further. Jesus captured the importance of relationships with his two key points: Love God and love your neighbor as you love yourself. We are social animals who can thrive only in being with others.

Dust to Dust

> The most courageous thing we will ever do is to bear humbly the full mystery of our own humanity and divinity—living as one with the One.
>
> —Richard Rohr

Many have said, and I totally agree, that we are first spiritual beings trying to be human beings. Even the word "person" means a sounding through—so, in essence, we are all spiritual beings sounding through to the world as humans. Our great challenge is to continue to learn how to look at one another and see that we are all the whole of God's creation.

I was taking my ten-year-old granddaughter to a ballet class and she brushed her hand across the interior console of the car and stared at the dust. She asked me, "Papa, where did this dust come from?" I answered with a smile, "Well, Virginia, it came from the same place we came from." (I had a sense she already knew about the "birds and the bees" so I didn't have to go there!)

She said, "Really? What does that mean?" So I told her that we came from the cosmic dust and that when we die we will return to dust. While we are alive we are filled with God's spirit in this temporary world and when we die we return to God's eternal world. The crazy and wonderful thing is that both this temporary life and our eternal life are filled with love. And that, Virginia, is why I love you.

The Paradox of Mortality

It is quite impossible for a thinking being to imagine nonbeing, a cessation of thought and life, in this sense, everyone carries the proof of his own immortality within himself.

—Goethe

Floating in our kayak downstream in later years, more and more often we look around and many of our journey companions are no longer there. Our culture does a good job of "sanitizing" death— removing from our everyday life the grisly details and maudlin narratives of dying. I noticed lately that I am frequently reading the obituaries to see if anyone I have known has been taken off the rivers of life.

The subject of death may be like a bank of dark clouds on the horizon that you occasionally stare at to see if they are advancing towards you. When a good friend calls us to share news of a recent cancer diagnosis, when another friend suddenly falls from a ladder and is buried three days later, the clouds appear to be closer and more terrifying.

We should not be surprised by death. As we drift downstream, we can see that everything around us changes, everything erodes or dies. Death's onslaught is relentless. Nature fights for life but does not resist dying. As a sentient being, we are the only species that struggles with the paradox of our own mortality. We are objectively aware that, like all other living things around us, we one day must die. Yet, our subjective minds cannot imagine a state of non-existence—it's inconceivable.

When my grandmother broke her hip and was living out her last days, I remember sitting by her bed and holding her hand. For the first time, she was sharing her deepest thoughts as she confronted her pending death. She said that she realized that her broken body would soon die and decay but her soul would "soar into the hands of God!" I asked her what that would be like and she turned to me and said that she didn't really know but it was going to happen, for sure. Some of us call that faith.

Afterword

Thank you for taking time to float along with me, reflecting on key themes and experiences that may enrich our lives in retirement. It is my hope that your own kayak (inner self) is balanced, buoyant, and bouncing with joy and confidence as you paddle through your own journey streams.

The vignettes have offered various ideas and principles to guide us along the way. Reflecting on these various life experiences has been rewarding and deepened my appreciation for the gift of life and the healthy relationships and love of my fellow companions.

Perhaps you would enjoy writing about your own experiences that circle around these themes. You can download a free study guide at www.churchpublishing.org/restreaming. This reflective exercise may sharpen your awareness and equip you with valuable inner resources as you continue your journey into the later years.

Some have called our later years "the golden ones," a time to harvest the experiences of our lives and resonate with generativity, meaning-making, and love. On the horizon we know that there will be sicknesses, hardships, and eventually a time to accept the ending of our human journey—leaving behind loved ones, families, and friends.

Isaac Watts, lifting up words from the Moses prayer of Psalm 90 in 1738, wrote the famous hymn "O God Our Help in Ages Past":

Time, like an ever rolling stream,
Bears all its sons away;
They fly, forgotten, as a dream
Dies at the opening day.

Time, like an ever rolling stream, will bear all of us away but it is our hope that our legacy will be the resilient and indomitable spirit of love that will continue to dwell in the hearts of those who remain. And . . .

Oh God, our help in ages past,
Our hope for years to come,
Be Thou our guard while troubles last,
And our eternal home.

Acknowledgments

I am indebted to everyone mentioned in these pages, my life experiences with them, their influence in directing my path, and our deep and meaningful relationships. Supportive friends and family have enriched my life and formed my spiritual journey over the past seventy-plus years of circling around the sun.

I am deeply grateful for the support and encouragement from my wife, Margaret, as I entered the currents of my retirement and began writing this book. She courageously offered herself as the first reader of my written reflections and guided me gently with sincere affirmations. And special thanks to our daughter, Maysey, and her generous and exquisite talents in providing sketches throughout the book.

I also would like to thank Davis Perkins, former publisher of Church Publishing Inc., who encouraged me to write this book and guided my "kayak" along the way with helpful suggestions and editing.

The net proceeds from the sale of this book will be directed to Saint Vincent's Centre in Haiti. This Episcopal school provides children with disabilities special opportunities, support, and resources to learn, grow, and reach their full potential in their young life's journey toward adulthood. Since my retirement, I have been honored to serve on the board of directors and work with a talented staff. Along with the help of numerous dedicated volunteers, we are building a better future for the children at St. Vincent's. You can learn more and even make a contribution by viewing the website: www.stvincentshaiti.org.